CW01498190

Original title:

The Search for Purpose and Snacks

Author: Lucas Harrington

ISBN HARDBACK: 978-1-80566-027-9

ISBN PAPERBACK: 978-1-80566-322-5

Paths of Flavor and Meaning

In a world of chips and dip,
People munch while they trip.
Searching for a reason, bold,
Crunchy snacks are worth their gold.

With each bite, we ponder deep,
Do we choose our snack or keep?
A donut's ring might show us way,
But nachos call on game day.

Nibbles of Inspiration

A pretzel twist, oh what a fate,
Takes the edge off hunger's weight.
In each crunch, a lesson learned,
Yet crumbs of wisdom feel well-earned.

Granola bars stacked so high,
In their chewy goodness, I rely.
They whisper tales of courage found,
While I munch without a sound.

Finding Focus in Fritter

In the morning, sweet delights,
Fritters come to bless my sights.
With powdered sugar on my hands,
Do dreams come true or just expand?

Taking bites of fried delight,
Searching for the next insight.
Maple syrup's sticky track,
Shows where truths may hold us back.

Reflections in a Cookie Jar

Peeking in a jar, I spy,
Chocolate chips like stars in sky.
Do they hold the secrets sweet?
Or just crumbs of things to eat?

Each cookie holds a story grand,
Baked and formed by loving hand.
As I nibble, thoughts appear,
Is this joy or just veneer?

Muffins and Meaning

In a world of flour and dreams,
I chase down baked good schemes.
With sprinkles high and frosting low,
Where wisdom lies, I'll surely go.

A muffin top, my guiding star,
It whispers truths from near and far.
Chocolate chips with messages sweet,
In every bite, a new heartbeat.

Edible Explorations

I wander trails of bread and butter,
In the quest, I gladly stutter.
A sandwich here, a taco there,
Each bite brings joy, I'm fully aware.

With donuts round and cookies square,
I ponder life's great culinary dare.
Mustard sun and ketchup moon,
I snack while humming a silly tune.

A Spoonful of Solace

When life gets tough, I grab a spoon,
For ice cream dreams, I swoon and croon.
A scoop of joy in every bowl,
Spreading love, it fills my soul.

With sprinkles dancing on my treat,
I find my rhythm, feel the beat.
Each flavor whispers, "Stay awhile,"
In every scoop, I find a smile.

Seeking the Sweet Spot

In search of joy, I roam the shelf,
Gummy bears, I play with myself.
A cookie monster's heartfelt plea,
Snack time is life's best mystery.

With licorice ropes and taffy strings,
I ponder what true happiness brings.
Each candy piece, a bright delight,
In sugar's warmth, I find my light.

Seekers of Spice

In a kitchen so bright, with pots piled high,
A spoon in my hand, I let out a sigh.
Chasing flavors like dreams, oh what a quest,
But my tacos just won't cooperate, at best.

I sprinkle some salt and whisper some fate,
Hoping my chili won't turn out late.
The cumin's a tease, it winks as it waits,
While my heart's set on nachos and cheese on my plates.

Cookies Crumbling into Wisdom

A cookie jar holds more than treats inside,
It gathers my thoughts, my dreams, and my pride.
But I munch on the crumbs, distracted and lost,
Each bite's a reminder of wisdom's real cost.

Chocolate chips wink, like stars in the night,
But my mind's in a scramble, I just want a bite.
With each cookie crumble, a lesson unfolds,
That life's sweetest moments are not bought or sold.

Savory Secrets

In my cupboard of wonders, I rummage and dig,
A potato, some garlic, a mystery gig.
I sip from my broth, like a scholar's fine brew,
Learning life's answers through flavors I chew.

I found wisdom in sautéing, it's true,
With each golden crisp, I remember what's due.
The secrets of carrots, the truths of a stew,
Reveal that delight can be hearty and new.

A Bite of Belief

In the land of popcorn, my hopes take flight,
Puffed kernels of wisdom, all buttery and bright.
I munch on conviction, a savory cheer,
With every sweet bite, my visions are clear.

My nachos are crunchy, my cola a fizz,
Each snack a reminder of the joy that it gives.
So I laugh through this feast, as I giggle and grin,
For every bite taken, new adventures begin.

Snacks of Serenity

In the pantry, I seek delight,
A chip's crunch is pure sunlight.
Chocolate whispers soft to me,
Guiding my soul, oh, can't you see?

Microwave popcorn pops with glee,
Dancing kernels, wild and free.
A cheesy puff, my heart takes flight,
Filling my dreams with every bite.

The fridge hums a tune divine,
Pickles and pie, oh, how they shine!
With each morsel, joy is found,
In snacks, I'm blissfully spellbound.

Finding Nourishment in Nuance

In the garden of munching joy,
I hunt for crumbs, oh, what a ploy!
A cookie crumbles under my gaze,
In sweet layers, my spirit sways.

Granola bars whisper my name,
In their wrappers, I find fame.
A crunch here, a crunch there,
With every bite, I float in air.

Tacos sing with zest and flair,
Crisp lettuce makes me dance in chair.
In each flavor, a life's nuance,
Grazing with glee, I twirl and prance.

Filling the Empty

My stomach rumbles like a drum,
A quest for goodies has begun.
Nachos pile high, dipped in cheese,
A mountain of snacks, oh, how they please!

Jellybeans rain like happy thoughts,
In candy land, I find my spots.
Kettle chips call with a crisp delight,
Filling the void, banishing blight.

Toasty crackers dance on my tongue,
With each crunch, I feel so young.
My bowl of popcorn, a joyous sea,
In every kernel, I find glee.

Fruits of Inquiry

In the aisles, I roam with glee,
Searching for fruits that speak to me.
Bananas bounce, and apples grin,
In their sweetness, adventures begin.

I ponder grapes and their treasure,
A raisin's squish brings me pleasure.
A peach, so fuzzy, whispers close,
In each bite, I reflect, I dose.

Tangerines burst like laughter bright,
Juicy segments, my heart takes flight.
Each snack a story, not just for fun,
In every bite, a quest begun.

Sprinkles of Significance

In a world of creamy frosting,
I ponder what I'm lost in.
Cupcakes speak of sweet intent,
But brownies hold a deeper bent.

I try to find what life's about,
While munching cookies, oh so stout.
A fortune cookie might reveal,
That donuts keep my zest ideal.

Life's a cake I bake with glee,
Filling it with sprinkles, just for me.
Each bite a clue, each nibble a sign,
Chocolate chips that intertwine.

So I laugh with each sweet treat,
Hoping for wisdom in every bite I meet.
Purpose served on a platter of fun,
With every morsel, I can run!

Dipping into Determination

With chips and guac, I dive right in,
Determination thick as sin.
Nachos stacked, a mountain high,
Searching for meaning nestled nigh.

A salsa swirl to heighten my quest,
In queso pools, I find some rest.
Each crunch declares a self-made fate,
As I dip before it's far too late.

Pretzel bites with a twist and turn,
Marking trails with each crisp churn.
On top of snacks, I'm riding free,
Finding purpose, one dip for me.

With every bite, I forge ahead,
Fueling dreams and crumbs I've spread.
In laughter and cheese, I draw the line,
Snackin' on life, feeling just fine!

Peanuts and Pathways

On a path of salted nuts,
I stumble on life's little ruts.
Underfoot, a trail of shells,
Each crunch a tale my spirit tells.

Walking wide with bags in hand,
Observing pathways, oh so grand.
Cashews whisper, "Take a chance,"
While almonds nod in nutty dance.

Life's a mix of sweet and salty,
With every snack, I feel more faulty.
Peanut butter spreads my dreams,
As jelly rolls in sweet extremes.

Finding purpose in every bite,
With every nugget of delight.
So I snack my way through every phase,
In laughter's light, I'll spend my days!

Fibers of Fate

In a world of loaves and grains,
I sift through laughter, flexing veins.
Whole wheat speaks of sturdy trails,
While bagels spin my fairy tales.

Fiber-rich and mighty fine,
Pasta shapes do intertwine.
Looking for a noodle's lore,
In every swirl, I find much more.

Popcorn kernels dance and pop,
Finding wisdom in each plop.
With butter drizzles on the side,
Through fluffy clouds, I choose to glide.

Purpose baked within each bite,
As snacks embrace with pure delight.
In every crumb, a truth awaits,
Fate is flavor, served on plates!

Spice-rack of Self

In the cupboard, spices wait,
Cilantro, cumin, more on their plate.
A dash of humor, a pinch of zest,
Who knew self-discovery could taste the best?

Thyme for reflection, salt for the soul,
Paprika dreams, making me whole.
A sprinkle of laughter, don't take it too hard,
Cooking my journey in a kitchen so charred.

Whisking away Doubts

With a whisk in hand, I take a stand,
Bouncing worries like a rubber band.
Eggs crack open, revealing my fears,
Whipped into fluff with laughter and cheers.

Add in the sugar, sprinkle in joy,
Stirring my doubts like an overcooked soy.
The batter's quite thick, but up goes my smile,
Mixing my thoughts with a dash of style.

Muffins of Meaningfulness

Muffins rise tall, with meaning inside,
Blueberries of wisdom, sweet wisdom to bide.
Each bite a lesson, each crumb a laugh,
Learning's delicious, cut the loaf in half!

The oven's my mentor, heat on high,
Flavor and purpose, oh my, oh my!
I sprinkle some laughter, sprinkle some fun,
Baking my path until day is done.

Pursuing the Palette

Colorful dreams on a plate I pursue,
A canvas of flavors, oh what a view!
Tasting the rainbow, each hue my guide,
Life's a buffet, come on, let's glide!

Fruits of the labor, veggies in line,
Sautéing ambitions, oh isn't it fine?
With forks of ambition, and spoons of delight,
Let's feast on the journey, from morning till night.

Salad of Dreams

In a bowl where greens collide,
I tossed my hopes with ranch inside.
Tomatoes danced, cucumbers leaped,
But still those dreams, they never steeped.

Croutons chattered, all in jest,
Claiming salad's where dreams rest.
But every bite, my thoughts would stray,
To pizza slices, come what may.

The dressing drizzled, quite a show,
Yet near the fridge, my cravings grow.
A bag of chips calls out my name,
In this leafy bowl, who feels the same?

So here I am, a veggie knight,
Yet cheese and bacon smell so right.
A crunchy quest ends not in greens,
But in the pantry's hidden scenes.

Crusts and Crossroads

At the corner where I stand and muse,
A slice of bread with hefty blues.
Peanut butter, jelly's grace,
But what if donuts call my race?

A crusty path, a flaky fate,
Should I indulge or try to wait?
Croissants croon their buttery song,
While I deliberate, it feels so wrong.

Sourdough whispers of ancient quests,
But sugar-laden wonders are my tests.
As pastries peddle their sweet embrace,
I contemplate my carb-filled space.

Oh, life's a crust, both soft and hard,
Navigating snacks feels like a card.
With every bite, I ponder deep,
The tastiest choice—my secret keep.

Stirred by Snacks

In the pantry, chaos strewn,
Chips and dips in afternoon.
A microwaved delight to tease,
While popcorn pops in gusty breeze.

My heart leaps at each salty sound,
As nachos crunch and cheese is crowned.
But in this party, what's my role?
Am I the host or just a troll?

Veggies whisper, 'We're so good!',
But snacks with zest, they know I would.
To dip or not, I stand and stare,
At crispy bites beyond compare.

So here's the riddle I must crack,
What's fulfilling—bowl or snack?
The answer's clear, it lights my way,
Savor each crunch and laugh all day!

Bread as a Beacon

In the kitchen, a loaf rays bright,
With butter spread, it feels just right.
A beacon in the foodie night,
I chase its warmth, what a delight!

With each slice, a path unfolds,
A crusty tale, adventure holds.
Should I slather it with jam?
Or pair with meats? Oh, woe, oh, slam!

The joy of dough, it calls my name,
Fueling whims, igniting flame.
Still fond of crumbs that leave their mark,
Yet cheese and wine, they play the lark.

So here I stand, with butter knife,
Deciding crumbs or zest for life.
Each bite a journey, bliss and cheer,
Together we snack, without a fear!

Crunchy Contemplations

In a world of chips and dips,
I ponder my own snack trips.
Do I seek the crunch divine,
Or just a reason to dine?

A cookie asks, 'What's your plan?'
A pickle says, 'Be a fan!'
Potato waves with a grin,
'Join me, let's begin to win.'

With nachos piled high and proud,
I wonder, can snacks be a crowd?
Yet, one lone carrot sticks around,
Sighing softly, 'I'm still astound.'

So I munch with delight and glee,
Contemplating chips and me.
As crumbs dance in lost reflection,
Isn't this snack time perfection?

Whispers of Wonder and Waffles

A waffle twirls with syrup dreams,
What life is this, or so it seems?
It whispers sweetly, 'Join the fun,
For breakfast melts under the sun!'

Pancakes flip with a curious frown,
'Why do you ponder while we drown?'
A butter pat rolls on its side,
'The secret's within, just flutter and glide!'

The toaster pops with a cheerful sound,
'What purpose do you seek around?'
'Just crispy edges and warm delight,
Waffles giggle, 'It feels just right!'

So I savor each golden bite,
Lost in soft warmth and tasty light.
With giggles shared, I wave goodbye,
To breakfast dreams as they float by.

Savoring Silence in the Soul

In a quiet room, I munch alone,
With popcorn kernels gently sown.
I ponder life's great mystery,
And munch with glee, a sight to see!

A donut sighs with glazed content,
As I take time for each ascent.
'What's the meaning behind my glaze?'
I grin and nibble through the haze.

A chocolate chip drops in dismay,
'To be devoured, that's my way!'
The silence speaks between each bite,
As crumbs of joy take flight at night.

Oh, to munch my way to bliss,
Finding truth in every miss.
Savoring silence, sweet and whole,
As snacks connect deep in my soul.

Bites of Bliss on the Journey

As I stroll through a pantry vast,
Searching for goodies, oh what a blast!
A granola bar calls, 'Take a chance!'
Shall I indulge in a snacky dance?

With each bite, life's troubles fade,
A gummy bear joins in the parade.
'Why chase dreams when you can chew?'
I ponder this with just one view.

Chips crunch softly, sharing tales,
Of journeys bright and buffet trails.
Each bite's a chapter, sweet and bold,
Eating my way through stories told.

So I gather the taste and cheer,
Life's purpose seems so very near.
With each morsel, I laugh and sing,
Bites of bliss—the joy they bring!

Bites of Ambition

In the cupboard, dreams reside,
With chips and cookies, side by side.
I chase my goals, but where's the pie?
Snack goals make my ambitions fly.

I set my sights on fruit and grain,
But find my heart in pizza's reign.
A salad whispers sweetly, 'Hey!'
Yet pizza beckons, 'Come and play!'

With every crunch, my spirits lift,
In nachos, I find my true gift.
In trials tough, I munch my way,
For joy comes wrapped in a buffet.

So I shall soar on cheddar wings,
Chasing after all good things.
With every bite, my heart ignites,
In life's great feast, I claim my rights!

The Journey of a Scone

Once upon a time, a scone did dream,
To rise above tea, the perfect team.
With butter, jam, and visions grand,
A flaky quest, not as simple as planned.

Through kitchens hot and winds that blew,
A quest for glaze, the scone pursued.
''Twas not just crumbs that gave me hope,
But sprinkles, sugar, to help me cope.

With raspberry filling and a crumbly core,
I sought a picnic and so much more.
But alas, a bee buzzed near my plate,
I left my dreams—then sealed my fate!

I stumbled, rolled, but never lost,
In every setback, learned the cost.
At last, on high tea's cherished end,
I found my purpose, had found a friend!

Curated Cravings

With every snack, I ponder deep,
Potato chips and wild dips I heap.
A gourmet blend of munchy dreams,
Each bite a laugh, or so it seems.

I strategize my cereal game,
Will it be sweet or slightly lame?
The granola's got my back all day,
While donuts cheer and say, 'Hooray!'

A fruit parade of colors bright,
led by gummy bears, oh what a sight!
Each craving curates joy and jest,
Who knew food quests could be the best?

So here I sit, with treats in hand,
A funny tale in snack-land planned.
Curated joys, with laughter spun,
Life's best moments, all wrapped in fun!

Navigating the Nosh

On a sea of wrappers, I set my sail,
With chips and dip, I cannot fail.
A treasure map of sweetness traced,
Through cookie dough, my dreams embraced.

I wave to pretzels, like ships at sea,
'Come join my picnic, just you and me!'
A soda fountain bubbles low,
As salty waves begin to flow.

The gummy sharks swim past the fries,
In this snacking quest, I wear a guise.
To navigate through crunchy quests,
I laugh and munch, it's just the best!

With each bold bite, my ship sets course,
For pudding cups and popcorn's force.
Through laughter and crumbs, I steer the mash,
In a crispy world, I'll make a splash!

Muffin Tops and New Heights

In a bakery bright, with treats all around,
I ponder my life, while muffins abound.
Exploring dimensions, both fluffy and round,
What's the meaning of life? I just need a pound!

With sprinkles and frosting, I whimsically quest,
Is purpose found here? I'm feeling quite blessed.
While nibbling my muffin, I've surely found zest,
Is icing the key? I must put it to test!

My coffee is strong, it fuels my delight,
As I munch and I crunch, I feel oh so right.
Perhaps joy is hidden in bites of pure white,
As I dream of the next cookie that's out of sight!

So let's toast to the life of a snack-loving sage,
With muffins and giggles, I turn a new page.
The flavors of joy become my true wage,
In this muffin top journey, I'm setting the stage!

Questing for Meaning and Munchies

With chips in my pocket and dip on my mind,
I wander through aisles, the best snacks to find.
Is that crunch of a potato where fortune is signed?
In the quest for a bite, pure wisdom aligned!

Should I dive into pretzels or savor a cheese?
Each choice that I make brings me closer to peace.
While pondering snacks, I truly am pleased,
For in every good bite, my worries do cease!

With each tasty morsel, I chew on my fate,
Is life just a buffet? I'm learning, feel great!
As I nibble more slowly, my heart seems to sate,
With laughter and munchies, I embrace my own plate!

So pass me the popcorn, I'm ready to chew,
In pursuit of the savory and flavors so true.
Between nachos and laughter, I find my own view,
In this march for good snacks, I'm perfecting my hue!

Crumbs of Clarity

In the crumbs of my cookie, I find hidden thoughts,
While chocolate chip secrets unravel like knots.
What wisdom lies waiting in each mouthful shot?
Is truth found in munchies? Oh, I may have caught!

I nibble on cake while I ponder my lot,
In layers of frosting, I connect every dot.
Is life like a buffet? A puzzle, a plot?
With crumbs of clarity, my worries are fought!

As I delve into snacks, my worries unwind,
Each bite is a moment that helps me not find.
In the mess of my munching, contentment is lined,
With laughter and flavor, my visions aligned!

So here's to the goodies that bring us to joy,
In pastries and cookies, no thoughts we'll destroy.
Morsels of wisdom, I happily employ,
In the crumbs of my snacks, I discover my ploy!

Breadcrumbs on the Path of Fulfillment

With breadcrumbs behind me, I stroll down the lane,
In search of deliciousness, simple yet plain.
Each bite is a step that guides me through pain,
As I munch on a roll, I feel joy in the grain!

The journey is sprinkled with savory treats,
From crackers to sweets, oh, life's little feats!
I gather my snacks like my life's little beats,
Through laughter and crumbs, I savor each seat!

As I crunch through the moments, I find something grand,

In the joy of the munching, I'm losing my bland.
With breadcrumbs to guide me, I make my own stand,
In this banquet of life, I'm just taking command!

So let's raise a donut to growth and to cheer,
In the quest for fulfillment, we chew without fear.
With each laugh and nibble, I find myself near,
In the crumbs and the giggles, my path becomes clear!

Confections of Contentment

In a world so vast and wide,
I seek my treats with pride.
Chocolate bars and fudge delight,
Keep me up long into the night.

Searching high and searching low,
For candy stashed, where did it go?
Life's sweet bliss, a sprinkle here,
A jellybean brings on the cheer.

With gummy bears and lollipops,
Each little bite, my heart just hops.
Add some ice cream, blend the fun,
Happiness is never done.

Crunchy, munchy, oh so great,
I'll never give up my snack plate.
In this quest, what do I find?
A happier heart, a playful mind.

Pairing Dreams with Dishes

I dream of fries on golden trays,
Along with gravy, crispy ways.
The burgers sing a siren call,
Together they dance, oh what a ball!

Lemon tarts and pies that shine,
Each dessert a tale divine.
Mixing flavors in a bowl,
Every bite ignites my soul.

In culinary fantasies I roam,
Pasta twirls, feels like home.
With every fork I take a chance,
On tasty bites, I start to prance.

Some call it madness, some call it fun,
As I savor every bun.
With each dish, my dreams take flight,
Pairing flavors feels just right.

Flavorful Footprints

Step by step, I wander wide,
With popcorn tucked on every side.
Each kernel popped, a trail I lay,
In this tasty game, I'll play!

A jelly donut, plump and round,
Marks the path where joy is found.
Chocolate sprinkles all around,
Each little bite does astound.

Muffin crumbs behind my feet,
Lemon bars that can't be beat.
With every nibble, every crunch,
Life's full of surprises for lunch.

So here I walk, with snack in hand,
Creating joy, just as I planned.
With every treat, my heart's aglow,
In this wild journey, let's go!

Grainy Tracks to Purpose

Sowed my dreams in cereal fields,
Flakes of hope, the crunch it yields.
To find my way, I munch and snack,
Discovering joy in every crack.

With bags of chips that guide my way,
And chocolate cookies bright as day.
I navigate through bites and tastes,
In this adventure, no time to waste.

Sushi rolls and taco treats,
Spicy, savory, oh so neat!
Each flavor leads me down a path,
Laughing hard, I feel the math.

From granola bars to peanut butter,
I crunch along with every utter.
In this journey, fun's the aim,
With every snack, I win the game!

Tasting Life's Mysteries

In the pantry I roam, is there meaning in chips?
Crispy crunch calls my name, like sweet little quips.
Each morsel a riddle, to chew and to bite,
Do snacks hold the answer to life's curious plight?

With each tasty treat, my quest takes a turn,
Flavors ignite, as my stomach will yearn.
Is it nachos or peanuts that bring forth delight?
Or maybe a donut, to thrill day and night?

I pluck at my choices, the muffin or cake,
Both promise sweet joy, neither one I can fake.
But how can I find, in this sugary dance,
The meaning of life tucked in butter and chance?

So I laugh at the search, with crumbs on my chin,
Life's treasures unearthed when you dive in and grin.
In flavors so funny, I wander and snack,
Finding purpose in bites, there's no looking back!

Gains from Grains

Grains fill the shelves, but what do they mean?
Oats in my bowl, a wholesome routine.
Each spoonful a puzzle wrapped up in a bowl,
But really, is fiber the key to my soul?

Rice cakes in hand, I crunch with a grin,
Do they hold the secrets? Should I dive in?
Cornflakes dance lightly, with milk they collide,
Am I gaining wisdom, or just getting fried?

Nature's own marvel, the bread and the rolls,
Can they guide my path, like magical scrolls?
A bagel with cream cheese, a treasure I crave,
But is it a purpose or breakfast I save?

Through muffins and crackers, I stumble and munch,
Exploring the universe, one crouton for lunch.
With humor I nibble, in each grainy bite,
Finding joy in the mundane, it all feels so right!

A Chewy Path Forward

Gumdrops and licorice pave my long way,
Each chew a decision, come join in the play.
Caramels sing sweetly, as I ponder my fate,
Is this chewy journey just sugar on plate?

Taffy pulls gently, like life's little strings,
Will I stretch for my dreams, or just savor the things?
A gummy bear winks with a wink and a smile,
Should I nap or adventure? Let's chew for a while.

Be careful with bites, they may glue you in thought,
Like life's sticky choices, are they worth what I sought?
Each morsel a fork, in this candy-coated maze,
Biting off more, or is it wisdom I praise?

So here on my chewy path, I bounce and I sway,
With laughter and laughter, in a sugary play.
No matter the answers in this sticky parade,
It's the fun in the journey that simply won't fade!

Flavors of Wholeness

A fruit basket waits, with colors so bright,
Bananas and berries dance under the light.
Could these be the markers of life's tasty quest?
As I munch on my mango, I feel truly blessed.

Nutty delights, bursting out of their shell,
A hint of adventure and tales they could tell.
Here's to the almonds and cashews that shine,
In this flavorful journey, it's all SO divine!

Veggies aplenty, with crunches galore,
Carrots and peppers, who could ask for more?
Dipped in a dressing, or maybe just raw,
Every bite's a delight, can you feel the awe?

With laughter and spice, I savor my plate,
Life's flavors remind me that there's never too late.
In the quest for wholeness, I find joy in my snacks,
Each bite tells a story, and I'll never relax!

The Flavorful Pursuit of Meaning

In kitchens bright, we seek delight,
A quest for joy, both day and night.
With spatulas raised and pots ablaze,
We hunt for flavors in our maze.

Cookies crumbled, wisdom stirred,
In frosting dreams, our thoughts are blurred.
What's life without a tasty bite?
Grab a donut, hold on tight!

Between the stocks and simmered stew,
We ponder deep, just me and you.
Is avocado toast the key to bliss?
Or maybe pizza? Can't dismiss!

So let's embrace this savory ride,
With whipped cream clouds and giggles wide.
For in each crumb of cake we munch,
Is secret sauce, the best for lunch!

Tastes of Truth and Tedium

In bowls of cereal, truths are found,
Each crunch reveals what's lost and sound.
A spoonful of chaos, tossed with glee,
Why is breakfast the strangest spree?

With every nibble, questions brew,
Is chocolate really good for you?
As we debate with guacamole,
Life's best lessons come unholy!

Snack time laughs fill the air with jokes,
As chips collide with hungry folks.
We crunch and munch, unmask the lies,
In sour cream, our wisdom lies.

Find your truth among the fries,
Sometimes purpose is greasy surprise.
With every bite, embrace the grind,
Tedium fades, joy's what we find!

Beyond the Plate: A Journey Within

Past the pita and hummus dip,
We search for meaning on a trip.
In every forkful, stories dwell,
Just beyond the pasta shell.

Cabbage rolls and tales unfold,
In every spice, a truth is sold.
What's the meaning of coleslaw?
A deeper cry or merely raw?

Beneath the cheese, a world awaits,
With every nibble, life debates.
A cosmic crunch, a crispy cheer,
Answers served with extra beer.

So as we dine, let laughter pour,
On icy treats, we'll leave a score.
Search within the tasty layers,
Find your path in sweet conveyors!

Culinary Curiosities of the Heart

With spatula heart, we take a stand,
Flipping pancakes on demand.
In syrup rivers, dreams awake,
What's the purpose in this cake?

A cookie's crunch can heal the soul,
While ramen fills that hungry hole.
In every bite, a love affair,
With nachos, cheese, and midnight flare.

Let our palates dance with glee,
As we taste life, just you and me.
With pickles sweet and fries so bright,
Who knew the heart could take a bite?

So laugh and munch with all your might,
In savory snacks, we find the light.
Explore the flavors near and far,
In every dish, we find who we are!

Crumbs of Clarity

In a pantry so deep, I embark with glee,
Searching for treats that are waiting for me.
The cookies are crumbly, the chips are so loud,
A feast of delight makes me feel quite proud.

With each little bite, confusion unravels,
The taste of each snack navigates through the travails.
So I munch and I crunch, finding humor in crumbs,
These little delights are life's simple sums.

A snack in each hand ignites my sweet quest,
With every new flavor, I feel truly blessed.
Still lost in thought, my tummy does sigh,
For purpose and pastries, I'll always comply.

So here's to the snacks that bring joy from within,
Each bite is a laugh, let the feasting begin!
No need for grand wisdom when chips are so near,
I'll find my path forward, with snacks and some cheer!

Dreams in Every Bite

In a world made of snacks, I dare to believe,
That every small morsel holds dreams to weave.
A chocolate bar's promise, a cookie's sweet giggle,
Is life's little riddle, with laughter to wiggle.

As I munch on some pretzels, I ponder and chew,
Is purpose just crumbs or a light crispy dew?
With every soft bite, my worries take flight,
Inside the realm of snacks, all feels so right.

So I dip into dips, and I crunch with delight,
Exploring each flavor, a rewarding night.
The laughter it brings, like melted fondue,
In this feasting and fun, I find wisdom anew.

With munchies in tow, I journey through dreams,
Finding purpose in flavors, or so it seems.
So here's to the snacks that tickle my soul,
In the pursuit of good times, they make me feel whole!

Whimsical Wonders and Warm Breads

In a land where muffins dance with glee,
And croissants sing sweet symphonies,
The toast waves hello, a golden hue,
While jelly dreams of a life anew.

The kitchen's alive with a cookie race,
Brownies giggle, it's quite the place.
With sprinkles on cupcakes, a party unfurls,
As the donuts spin in sugary swirls.

A pie in the corner winks with delight,
Baking's a sport, with flour in flight.
Scones in the oven unleash their cheer,
Raising a toast—oh, what a feast here!

With every bite, joy fills the air,
Carrot cake wishes for no one to share.
In this whimsical kitchen, laughter's the key,
Where everything's tasty, oh let it be free!

Revelations from the Pantry

In the depths of the pantry, things shift and sway,
Canned beans look mischievous, ready to play.
Pasta pirouettes, oh what a sight,
While rice grains plot a culinary flight.

"Just add some sauce!" a wise bottle calls,
As spices and herbs have fun at the balls.
The popcorn kernels are bouncing around,
While granola bars form a band with a sound.

Jars of jam gossip, sharing old tales,
While biscuits tell stories of sweet buttery gales.
A cheese block fancies itself quite refined,
As crackers compete to steal the spotlight, aligned.

With laughter and joy, the snacks take their place,
In this pantry jubilee, a loving embrace.
For in every munch, there's a moment of bliss,
A treasure of flavors, oh how could we miss?

Chasing Wholesome Whimsy

In a garden of veggies where laughter grows,
Carrots chuckle as a beet just dozes.
Tomatoes prance, round and so bright,
While peas in their pods hold secrets so tight.

A mischievous lettuce starts spinning around,
To the rhythm of forks and spoons' joyful sound.
Radishes roll, with quite the flair,
In this whimsical chase, they twirl in the air.

"Snack time!" they shout, "Let's make it grand!"
With laughter and crunch from every hand.
A symphony of flavors in baskets they twine,
In the land of delight where all snacks align.

With each crunchy bite, the merriment flows,
As the world turns savory, anything goes.
In a chase for the fun, let's dance and unite,
For wholesome whimsy brings pure delight!

Finding Flavor in the Fray

In a world of endless munch,
I seek the crunch of chips for lunch.
With each bite, my spirit soars,
As flavors dance and laughter roars.

A donut here, a cookie there,
I wander through the tasty fair.
Life's chaos fades in sweet delight,
When chocolate bars come into sight.

What's a goal without a snack?
A journey without taste is whack!
I ponder meaning in the cream,
Searching for that perfect dream.

So here I sit, my snack in hand,
With cheesy puffs, I take a stand.
In every crunch, I find my way,
For joy and flavor save the day.

Snacks of Solace

When troubles rise and chips are low,
I find my peace in nacho flow.
Pizza's warmth, a hug so tight,
In each slice, I see the light.

The world may spin, but here I pause,
Focusing on my snack-filled cause.
A bowl of nuts, a scoop of dip,
In every bite, I let it rip.

Chocolate bars, they offer grace,
In moments lost, I find my space.
Through salty waves and sweet escapes,
I chew through life, embracing shapes.

With every crunch, a giggle shared,
The laughter rings, the world is bared.
In simple joys, I find my claim,
For snacks of solace fuel the flame.

Chewing on Life's Mysteries

I ponder life with peanut fries,
As burger bites illuminate the skies.
Each spicy nugget tastes divine,
A riddle wrapped in cheesy brine.

What's hidden in the cookie's core?
A treasure map or crumbs galore?
I dunk my thoughts in milk anew,
As donut holes bring clarity, too.

With every crunch, a truth unfolds,
In nacho tales, the heart beholds.
A crispy chip, a fortune read,
Life's mysteries solved in crumbs of bread.

So let's embrace the snacky spree,
In flavors bold, we find the key.
For every laugh and bite I take,
Unravel life, for friendship's sake.

Reflections Stirred by Snacks

In the kitchen, I embark on quests,
A cereal box - oh, what a jest!
With milk like rivers, I float along,
In breakfast bliss, I find my song.

Popcorn bursts, a fluffy cheer,
As movies play, it's loud and clear.
With caramel drizzles and flavors bold,
I savor stories, both new and old.

Potato chips whisper secrets sweet,
In crunches loud, our hearts do meet.
Through every nibble, humor flies,
As salty tears meet cheesy highs.

So raise your snacks, let laughter ring,
In every nibble, joy we bring.
With each delight, we find our way,
In tasty moments, the heart will play.

Grazing on Life's Lessons

In a field of dreams, I roam with glee,
Chasing down wisdom, like a wild spree.
With nachos in hand and a grin on my face,
Life's little lessons, I'm ready to chase.

I nibble on laughter, I munch on the fun,
Each silly mistake makes the process well done.
Pizza slices teach, and donuts do too,
Who knew my growth came with extra cheese goo?

With every bold bite, I savor the chance,
To waltz with my worries, to giggle and dance.
Hot wings and dreams, they both make me fly,
Each topping a lesson, I'm ready to try.

So here's to the snacks, and to all that they bring,
Each crumb a reminder that we're all just winging.
With chips in my purse and a twinkle in eye,
I'm grazing on life, and I'm never too shy.

Pastries and Pursuits

In the land of pastries, I hunt for the prize,
Croissants and cookies, a feast for the eyes.
With frosting in hand and sprinkles that gleam,
I chase after dreams like a sugary dream.

Donuts on a mission, they lead me so well,
Towards goals that are sweet, like a candy-filled shell.
I pledge my allegiance to pie and tarts rare,
In the quest for my passion, I lighten my chair.

Glazed with ambition and filled with delight,
Each bite tells a story, I savor the night.
Cheesecakes of wisdom, oh how they do call,
They whisper of triumphs, of rise and of falls.

So let's rise with the pastries, let's gallivant bold,
For in every sweet treat, there's a lesson retold.
With flour in my hair and joy in my heart,
I'm chasing my dreams, it's a whimsical art.

Breadcrumbs to Destiny

With crumbs in my pocket, I wander the way,
Each flake a reminder, come what may.
Chasing down breadcrumbs, I'm off to explore,
My destiny sprinkled in flour and more.

A muffin of fate, a cookie of chance,
Each morsel a giggle, inviting a dance.
With jelly and laughter, I spread it around,
In the banquet of life, joy is profound.

The crusty old loaf shows me how to knead,
While muffins proclaim that we're not just a feed.
Sourdough of wisdom, rise up from the past,
As I munch on my journey, a feast unsurpassed.

So here's to the crumbs that guide me each day,
In this playful little game, I laugh as I sway.
With snacks on my path and a grin ear to ear,
I'll dance with these offerings, spreading good cheer.

Applesauce and Aspirations

In a bowl of aspirations, I swim with a grin,
With applesauce dreams, let the laughter begin.
I dip into goals, with a spoonful of zest,
Finding sweet purpose in every bold quest.

Cinnamon whispers that life is a treat,
As I plot my own journey with apples to eat.
Each scoop brings me closer, oh what a delight,
In the sauce of ambition, everything feels right.

From soapy old kitchens to orchards afar,
I blend all my efforts and reach for the star.
With pie crusts of courage, I bake out my fears,
As I serve up my dreams with a side dish of cheers.

So let's savor the flavor of all that we chase,
With applesauce smiles, we'll make our own space.
In this journey of snacks, let's giggle and play,
For the sweetness of life is just one bite away.

Layers of Life's Cake

In a world of frosting bright,
We chase the layers, pure delight.
Sometimes it's chocolate, sometimes plain,
With every slice, there's more to gain.

Beneath the icing, secrets hide,
A sprinkle here, a candied ride.
Life's a buffet, so take a bite,
Find your slice of joy tonight.

Forks in hand, we take our stand,
The frosting helps, our dreams are planned.
Eating layers, made with care,
Fill your plate, if you dare!

Laughing crumbs fall from our chin,
Try a flavor, let the fun begin.
In each layer, a story's spun,
Grab a piece, and share the fun!

Trail Mix for the Soul

Nuts and chocolate, a happy blend,
Each munch is magic, a tasty trend.
With every trail, we find our cheer,
The sweetest bites bring us near.

A raisin here, a candy there,
Mix it up, we have no care.
Through crunchy paths, our hearts will soar,
Life's a hike with snacks galore.

Joy is found in bits and bytes,
Savoring flavors, scaling heights.
For every trek, a handful's treat,
With every crunch, we find our beat.

So grab your bag, don't be shy,
On this adventure, let's fly high.
In every crunch, a giggle waits,
Snack on, my friend, life's what creates!

Savoring Simple Joys

A cookie crumb, a giggle shared,
In simple moments, love declared.
Laughter spills like warm milk flow,
In tiny bites, our spirits grow.

A sip of tea, a sunny day,
Every little joy lights the way.
With friends around, we toast and cheer,
Savoring life, and snacks so dear.

A slice of pie, a cheerful tune,
Melodies dance like a bright balloon.
With every laugh, our hearts align,
In every bite, the world's divine.

Hold on tight to each small bliss,
For in this life, it's joy we miss.
Snack on sweetness, laugh out loud,
In simple joys, we're rich and proud!

Pies of Potential

In an oven warm, dreams arise,
Golden crusts beneath the skies.
Each pie a hope, each filling a dream,
A scoop of "yes," a dash of cream.

Flavors twirl like whims of fate,
Lemon zest on our dinner plate.
With every slice, we dare to try,
Pies of potential make spirits fly.

Chocolate cream, or blueberry bliss,
Each little bite, a moment to kiss.
Whip cream mountains on top await,
Life's delicious when we celebrate.

Gather round, with laughter's ring,
Share the goodness that baking brings.
In every bite, we find our call,
Pies of potential, they'll conquer all!

Seeking Substance in Shredded Wheat

In a box with a smile, I dive in deep,
Looking for wisdom where fibers creep.
Each crunch is a question, a riddle to crack,
Is this wheat my wisdom or just a snack?

I ponder the fibers, the grains that I munch,
Do they hold the key, or just serve as lunch?
With each bite I giggle, a thought comes to me,
Maybe purpose is fluff, like my cereal spree.

The milk pours like dreams, so creamy and bright,
I mix up a potion, my mind takes flight.
In a bowl swirling laughter, I float on the waves,
Happiness found in the crunch of my saves.

So here's to my morning, with brisk little bites,
Where wisdom gets lost in the cereal sights.
Though the quest may seem silly, I'll munch and I'll play,

Finding joy in the crunch as I start my new day.

Cherishing Each Cracker

Tiny squares stacked high, a tower of glee,
Each bite a reminder, of what's fun to be.
With cheese or alone, in a warm, cozy wrapper,
I relish my moment, oh what a good capper!

I dip, I spread, I take a big crunch,
Every shape and flavor, it's a satisfying lunch.
Bitter or sweet, no cracker gets left,
In the kingdom of snacks, they're all truly deft.

A corner of crispness, a dash of delight,
In my snack time carnival, they take off in flight.
They chirp and they laugh, in the box where they dwell,
Each cracker a secret, a story to tell.

So cherish each nibble, don't cast them aside,
In the quest for the crunchy, there's no need to hide.
For in every crisp morsel, a sparkle does bloom,
A dance of deliciousness lights up the room.

Fulfillment in Flavors

A swirl of the sauces, a dip far and wide,
I crack open bags, with joy as my guide.
Every flavor a dream, each chip holds a tale,
In the land of the tasty, no palate will ail.

I sprinkle some spice, a dash of delight,
As flavors collide in a fanciful bite.
With nacho, and salsa, and guacamole jam,
I build my own world where I feel like a champ.

The crunch echoes laughter, the salsa does sway,
In the harmony of flavors, I frolic and play.
There's zest in my journey, with every taste bud,
A rainbow of spices, a colorful flood.

So here's to my munchies, my flavorful quest,
In the crunch of my cravings, I always find best.
For when flavors unite, there's a party at hand,
And fulfillment in snacks is a reason to stand.

Unwrapping Possibilities

Wrapped tight like my dreams, in colors so bright,
A snack can inspire from morning to night.
Each layer I peel back, reveals treasures anew,
In the world of my munchies, there's always a clue.

With wrappers like puzzles, I'll take up the game,
Every foil and paper, the snacks call my name.
A crunch here, a squish there, the flavors align,
In the riddle of snacking, the answers are mine.

From chips to candies, the options so vast,
In a universe tasty, forever to last.
I ponder the snacks, what joy can unfurl,
As I delve into snacks, life whirls and twirls.

So unwrap those delights, let curiosity spark,
In the garden of munchies, ignite up the dark!
For in the fun of the hunt, where flavors all gleam,
The path to pure joy is a sugary dream.

Nourishing the Spirit with Nibbles

In the fridge, I find some bites,
A cheese that squeaks, oh what delights!
I ponder life with every crunch,
As pickles dance, I have my lunch.

The cookies whisper sweetly low,
While chips engage in a salty show.
I seek the path that leads to fun,
With each new flavor, I'm never done.

Exploring Existence through Treats

I wander aisles of crunchy bliss,
Searching for that perfect kiss—
Of frosting, sprinkles, and some cake,
The epiphany's just a bite to take.

Between the bites of fudge and pie,
I question why the donuts fly.
Purpose found in every scoop,
As chocolate chips make a happy group.

Delightful Dilemmas and Dumplings

Should I dive for dumplings or sushi rolls?
My heart is torn in tug-of-war polls.
With every dip in soy or sauce,
I lose myself; oh, what a loss!

The options spread like wide-open skies,
With fortune cookies full of surprise.
Each bite unlocks the mysteries,
While food rejoices, brings me glee!

Morsels of Motivation

I nibble on my dreams like treats,
Each morsel shines, a joy that beats.
A peanut butter toast of fate,
Crusty crumbs that animate!

As pretzels twist and stories flow,
I find my reason in the dough;
From gummy bears to velvety pie,
With snacks, my hopes can truly fly!

Unraveling Mysteries with a Side of Fries

In a land where burgers roam,
I ponder life and munch alone.
With ketchup pools like deep concerns,
While fries perform their crispy turns.

Each bite a riddle, crispy, hot,
Is this what's meant by 'Thank you, pot'?
A shake of salt, a wink from fate,
Perhaps my purpose's on a plate.

A golden fry, a wise old sage,
What did I learn from this hot page?
I shrug, dip deep, and take a bite,
Maybe I'll know by dinner's light.

A Feast for the Mind

If thoughts were beans and dreams were cheese,
I'd construct a feast with perfect ease.
A taco built on whims and woes,
With guac to smooth the roughest prose.

Amidst the nachos stacked so high,
I question truth while munching pie.
Each crispy chip, a clue in disguise,
Unwrap the layers, hear the cries.

So here I sit with snacky aims,
Digesting hope through cheesy games.
In chips I trust; in dips, I thrive,
To feast on thoughts and feel alive.

Cookie Crumbs and Cosmic Questions

A cookie crumbles, secrets spill,
Each nibble brings a tiny thrill.
With chocolate chips like stars so bright,
I muse on life and every bite.

Why do we bake when questions rise?
Is flour dust to hide the spies?
Milk on the side, a truth revealed,
With crumbs like dreams that fate concealed.

I chase those crumbs of wisdom fair,
Through frosted peaks, I claw and tear.
But all I find are bites and sighs,
Perhaps the answers are in pies.

Seeking Serenity in Sweetness

In the search for bliss, I wield a spoon,
While ice cream whispers, 'Come, make room!'
Each scoop a prize, a creamy cheer,
With sprinkles bright, they draw me near.

I ponder why we crave the sweet,
Chocolate rivers flow beneath my feet.
Whipped cream clouds float overhead,
In this dessert, my thoughts are fed.

I'm scooping dreams with marshmallow swirls,
Searching for light as sweetness unfurls.
In every cone, the laughter flows,
It's in these treats my purpose grows.

Transformative Taffy

In a store of delights, I found a treat,
A taffy so bright, it's hard to beat.
Stretched and pulled, my mind did ignite,
Could sugary bliss lead me to light?

With each chew, a lesson, oh so sweet,
Like life's little puzzles, it's hard to cheat.
Some flavors explode, others fall flat,
Can candy be wisdom? Time to chat!

Twisting and turning, this taffy, my guide,
Unraveled my thoughts, like a wild ride.
In flavors of lemon, with hints of despair,
I pondered my purpose, did I really care?

But laughter erupted, as I chomped and chewed,
What matters more? It's the mood that ensued!
So here's to the taffy, my friend sincere,
A sugary journey, let's give a cheer!

Flavorful Fables

Once a banana with dreams, so bright,
Longed for adventures, to join the flight.
In a salad, in a pie, oh what a scene,
Living big dreams, but stuck in between.

An apple chimed in, with a crisp little grin,
"Why not just roll? Don't you want to spin?"
They pondered and laughed, as fruits often do,
In a basket of fate, they flew and they flew.

The kiwi suggested a trip to the fair,
With cotton candy clouds and popcorn to spare.
Purpose be sweet, but laughter's the goal,
Fables of flavor will tickle the soul!

So the fruits banded together, a quirky crew,
They danced on the table and sang songs anew.
In their fruity fables, they found their delight,
Purpose is fun, and oh what a sight!

Truffles of Truth

In a box of truffles, rich secrets reside,
Each bite, a mystery, I can't seem to hide.
With chocolate and toppings, they whisper to me,
'What truth do you seek? Just savor and be!'

A caramel swirl promised dreams made of gold,
While dark cocoa tales left my senses uncontrolled.
With laughter and giggles, I shared with a friend,
The truths of the truffles seem never to end.

Yet in each sweet morsel, a life lesson glows,
Some nuts are quite crunchy, while others are prose.
Clearly, existence's a mix, as I know,
With flavors and textures, we endlessly grow!

So I'll nibble on wisdom, with chocolate to share,
In wrappers of life, we handle with care.
Truths wrapped in sweetness—oh what a bond,
With truffles of wisdom, our spirits respond!

Chewing on Existence

Bubbly gum blows bubbles, spinning high,
Each pop brings a riddle, as time passes by.
With flavors of mint, I ponder and chew,
Is life just a flavor, or more like a stew?

The world, like my gum, is sticky and new,
Finding my rhythm with each little chew.
With bursts of cherry and sprinkles of zest,
I laughed at my worries, they weren't so compressed.

In this gum-chewing journey of twists and turns,
I fumbled and fumbled, but oh how I learned!
Existence may wobble, like a bubble on air,
But humor's my toolkit; it's everywhere!

So I'll chew on my thoughts, with joy I will find,
The quirks and the giggles that life leaves behind.
With each little chew, I'll keep making space,
For laughter and sweetness, a joyful embrace!

Refined Revelations

In the pantry's embrace, I seek my muse,
A box of donuts, or maybe some booze.
But every time I reach for a bite,
I ponder my life—while munching—it's right!

With each sweet morsel, I find my way,
In frosting and sprinkles, I revel and play.
A fork in the road, or a muffin to share,
Reminds me that laughter is free, always there!

So I'll dance with desserts and embrace the zest,
Each cookie a gem, each brownie—best fest.
With giggles and crumbs strewn all 'round my chair,
I find joy in foods that float in the air!

So onward I munch till the dawn meets dusk,
With delights that abound, without any husk.
For life's a grand banquet, each bite is a clue,
To the silly path I'm forging anew!

Crackerjack Certainty

In the depths of my cupboard, treasures await,
Salted pretzels, or popcorn that's great.
Each crunch a reminder to lighten my load,
As I ponder my fate and which snack to goad.

Cheese puffs whisper, they've got my back,
While celery sticks nibble, they've got no knack.
But that sugar rush, oh what a delight,
Turns my sorrow to giggles, from morning to night!

With each chip I devour, I toss out the woes,
Like birdseed, they're scattered, and up my joy goes.
The search is essential, though laughter's the prize,
In a universe filled with these edible skies!

So let me indulge, as I seek and I snack,
Life's a buffet, nothing's kept from my pack.
Crackerjack messages from snacks far and wide,
Guide me through mischief, with chips by my side!

Cake Layers of Life

Fondant and frosting, a spectacle bright,
Each layer I cut shows both day and night.
So I ponder my dreams with icing galore,
While devouring cake is what I truly adore!

Between chocolate and vanilla, I pause for a sec,
Life's flavors are blended, a delicious trek.
Sprinkles like stars across buttercream seas,
Where laughter is whipped cream—oh, how it frees!

So I stack all my layers, with gusto and glee,
A cake for each moment, come join in with me!
For the knife is my compass, my fork is the map,
As I navigate life through frosting and flap!

In this sweet adventure, I savor each bite,
With crumbs in my laughter, all wrong feels so right.
From cupcakes to chaos, I'll soar on this ride,
With cake as my beacon, my purpose my guide!

In Search of Sweet Surrender

Licorice whispers, "Come take a dive,"
While gummy bears giggle, all jived and alive.
The quest for the treat leads me here and there,
As marshmallows swell with a fluffy flair!

I chase down the sugar, my heart races fast,
Each bonbon a memory, a sweetness to last.
Chocolate cascades like a waterfall's flow,
In this candy world, I'm free to just glow!

The pie sings a ballad, the tart hums a tune,
As I plunge through dessert realms, my spirit's in bloom.
With brownies like clouds and whip cream that swirls,
I find both my purpose and joy in these pearls!

So here's to the treats that make life truly bright,
For within all the nonsense, there's savory light.
And as I revel in this sugary spree,
I discover my treasure, just my snack and me!

The Crunchy Conundrum of Being

Amidst the chips and salsa swirl,
I ponder life in a twirl.
Should I dip or should I crunch?
Oh, the thoughts that pack a punch!

In nacho cheese, my dreams do float,
With each bite, I'm on a boat.
Sailing through this cheesy maze,
Laughing hard in snacking craze.

Is it the taste or just the crunch?
I squirrel away a tasty bunch.
With every crumb, I seek a sign,
More salt? Or should I just unwind?

The conundrum's quite absurd,
Like choosing between truth or a bird.
But as I munch, I find my glee,
In crispy snacks, I'm truly free!

Munching Through Existential Quandaries

With popcorn's pop, I question life,
Is purpose close, or filled with strife?
Each kernel bursts with tasty glee,
Am I more salty or sweet, you see?

The cookie crumbles, oh, what a shame,
Yet chocolate chips recall my name.
Through each chew, I munch my fate,
In the brownie pan, I contemplate.

A fountain of fudge, my guiding star,
Do I need more? I think I do, by far.
With every bite, I feel the cheer,
Are snacks my purpose? It seems quite clear!

So here I sit with cake and pie,
Half-hearted thoughts as desserts fly by.
In marshmallow fluff, my dreams reside,
Eating my way through life's wild ride!

Pockets of Purpose and Pastries

With pockets deep, I stash my sweets,
Filled with doughnuts and other treats.
Purpose is found with every bite,
Sprinkled joy in the morning light.

Croissants whisper tales of the day,
Layer by layer, they melt away.
In buttery bliss, I search for signs,
Are these delights my true designs?

A muffin top holds wisdom vast,
With blueberry dreams and crumbs amassed.
I laugh aloud, a pastry quest,
Filling my heart with flaky zest.

So here I munch, my inner sage,
In frosting frolics, I find my page.
With cookies stacked, I chase my fate,
In every bite, I celebrate!

Riddles Served with a Side of Scones

Scones by the dozen, riddled in cream,
What is life's meaning? A sweet dream!
With every crumb, I sip my tea,
Is happiness found in blueberry?

The jam is sticky, like thoughts in my head,
Do I take a bite, or go back to bed?
Each flaky piece offers a clue,
In cinnamon swirls, I ponder anew.

The riddle's tricky, but I won't pout,
With laughter and pastry, I find my route.
Served warm and cozy, a delightful fate,
In every scone, I contemplate.

So let's debate with crumbs in tow,
Finding answers between bites, you know.
Life's puzzles dissolve like sugar in tea,
With scones by my side, I'm happy and free!

Revelations on a Platter

In the kitchen I roam, in search of delight,
A sandwich on toast, oh what a sight!
But mustard's too bright, it brings me dismay,
Yet chips on the side do brighten my day.

With each bite I take, I ponder and chew,
Is life just a snack, or something much true?
A pickle bittersweet, my thoughts start to swirl,
Does nacho cheese dip make sense in this whirl?

On Fridays I feast, in absolute bliss,
A cupcake or two is too sweet to miss!
A donut's my muse, it whispers my fate,
With sprinkles like stardust, oh how I love fate!

In laughter we gather, amidst crumbs and crumbs,
With cookies and milk, the joy always comes.
So let's raise a glass to the moments we find,
For snacks lead my heart to truths not defined.

Revelry in Rivels

Amidst the chaos of a dinner plate,
I munch on a snack, oh isn't it great?
Life tossed in laughs like chips in a bowl,
Seeking the crunch, it's good for the soul.

I chase after flavors, no time for a nap,
Zucchini on the table, oh what a trap!
With every new dip, my worries all fade,
A taco's bold charms, my troubles they trade.

With laughter we gather, our hearts in a stew,
Popcorn like magic, bright yellow and true!
Each story we share, is seasoned with cheese,
In this banquet of dreams, I snack with such ease.

So here's to the munchies, the giggles and grins,
In this quest for delight, oh where do we begin?
For flavored adventures and moments we crave,
In our bowl of life, it's fun that we save.

Flour Power and Fulfillment

Whisking away, flour dust in the air,
Searching for answers, handled with care.
A cupcake's soft whisper calls out from the rack,
With frosting like clouds, it means I'm on track.

In ovens so warm, ambitions arise,
But cookie dough tangles lead to sweet spies.
I bake and I ponder, is sugar the key?
To unraveling secrets, to living carefree?

With sprinkles like stars on my plate to behold,
I question the flavor, what stories unfold?
Each muffin a riddle, each brownie a clue,
Is happiness crumbled or served warm in stew?

So gather your forks, let's frolic, let's play,
With muffins and laughter, we'll savor the day.
Life's flour-coated moments are never a bore,
As I nibble on joy, I keep coming back for more.

Sweeten the Journey

On a winding path, I snack and I munch,
With chocolate round figures, it's quite the crunch!
In search for the giggle, I taste what I find,
A cookie's warm hug is the best for my mind.

With laughter like syrup drizzling down,
I chase after jellybeans, oh what a crown!
Life's twists and turns are sweeter in bites,
With marshmallows bouncing, oh what a delight!

As I wander and wonder, my backpack holds treats,
Tasting the joy as I stroll through the streets.
Candy-coated memories color my map,
In this journey of snacks, I find a warm lap.

So join in my quest, bring your own stash,
For savoring life does not need a pass.
With humor and flavor, let's dance hand in hand,
For life's all about zest, and a sprinkle of sand.